ENTREPRENEURSHIP FOR O-LEVEL

According to the new competency based curriculum as of 2020 for Uganda.

Ayebare Christopher

BBA, MBA-IB(Purs.)

First Published by

ISBN: 978-93-93385-98-7

Price: INR 150

BLUEROSE PUBLISHERS

www.bluerosepublishers.com

info@bluerosepublishers.com

Preface

Entrepreneurship is a solution to one of the major problems in Uganda that is unemployment, mostly in the youth population.

Through promotion of innovativeness and creative thinking so as to maximize available resources and opportunities for wealth creation.

Also encompasses other disciplines/subjects like commerce, accounts .

The book is organized into the following five chapters containing sub-chapters as follows;

Chapter 1: An entrepreneur, innovation, risks

Chapter 2: Businesses

Chapter 3: Business ideas

Chapter 4: Business start-up

Chapter 5: Government revenue

Suggestions for improvement in quality of the content are welcome.

Acknowledgement

I would like to extend my thanks to everyone that helped me in publishing this book.

I am also thankful to my parents, Dr Byakatonda Patrick, mrs Kyarisiima Rodah for their endless support towards me and my progression in everything.

They have not given up on me in any circumstances, life has thrown at me.

Lastly, I would love to thank the Almighty God for bringing me this far and always being by me whenever I need Him.

Ayebare Christopher

Contents

Chapter 1

Introduction to Entrepreneurship

1.1 WHO IS AN ENTREPRENEUR?

Definition

A person that identifies business opportunities and creates a new business venture is known as an entrepreneur.

They're characterized by their willingness to take risks, innovative thinking and the ability to adapt to changing market conditions.

They may operate in various sectors like technology, manufacturing, services among others.

For example: Elon Musk is an example of an entrepreneur because he has founded several companies like tesla and spaceX.

He has also paved way for new technologies like electric cars, re-usable rockets and underground transportation systems.

Another example is Mark Zuckerberg, the co-founder and CEO of Facebook, who started his entrepreneurial journey in college, developing a social networking platform that has grown to become one of the most widely used websites in the world.

1.2 MEANING OF ENTREPRENEURSHIP

Definition

Entrepreneurship is the process of creating, launching and running a new business venture that aims to provide innovative products or services that meet certain customer need or wants.

It is not limited to starting a new business, it can also involve innovation and creativity in existing businesses or organizations to bring new products or services to the market or improve existing processes and operations.

1.3 THE PURPOSE OF ENTREPRENEURSHIP EDUCATION

The purpose for this is to equip students with skills, knowledge and attitudes necessary to start and successfully operate their own businesses or engage in entrepreneurial activities.

Entrepreneurship education aims to instill the following;

i. **Entrepreneurial mindset**: Teaching of critical thinking and problem-solving skills prepares students to deal with new challenges and come up with innovative solutions.

ii. **Risk-taking**: Development of a mind-set that is open to take calculated risks in pursuit of their goals.

iii. **Creativity**: Entrepreneurship education also teaches students to think creatively which helps break traditional approaches in the marketplace.

iv. **Leadership skills**: Aims to develop leadership skills and the ability to inspire, motivate others.

v. **Financial skills**: It teaches students how to manage finances and secure funding as well.

Thus entrepreneurship-education is crucial in today's context as it plays an essential role in driving economic growth, innovation and job creation.

1.4 CHARACTERISTICS OF AN ENTREPRENEUR

Following are the major characteristics or features of an entrepreneur.

i. **Innovative thinking**: Entrepreneurs are highly innovative and creative. They possess the ability to think outside the box and develop unique ideas to challenge the status quo.

ii. **Risk taking**: They are willing to take calculated risks in pursuit of their goals. They understand that failure is part of the entrepreneurial journey and are willing to take risks to achieve success.

iii. **Passionate and committed**: They are willing to dedicate significant amounts of time, effort and resources to bring their ideas to reality.

iv. **Versatility**: They must be flexible thus adapting to different situations and challenges. They are quick to pivot and adjust their strategies as required to stay ahead of the competition.

v. **Strong work ethic**: Entrepreneurs have a strong work ethic and are willing to put in long hours to achieve their goals. They are self-motivated and driven to succeed.

vi. **Resilience and determination**: They must be able to bounce back from setbacks and stay motivated despite challenges.

vii. **Networking and relationship building**: They understand the importance of this thus have excellent communication and interpersonal skills and use them effectively to establish and nurture relationships with suppliers, customers and other stakeholders.

viii. **Visionary**: Entrepreneurs possess a visionary mindset, able to see the big picture and visualize the future. They are not afraid to dream big and work towards achieving their vision.

ix. **Adaptability**: They must be adaptive and open to change. They are always on the look-out for new opportunities and ways to improve their business.

x. **Financial services**: Must have strong financial skills, understanding the financial aspects of their business, and making sound financial decisions.

1.5 THE BENEFITS OF BEING AN ENTREPRENEUR

Some of the importance or benefits of being an entrepreneur include;

i. **Freedom**: As an entrepreneur, you have freedom to make your own decisions and control your own destiny. You have flexibility to work when and where you want.

ii. **Creativity**: Requires creativity and innovation, which can be a fulfilling and exciting experience.

iii. **Flexibility**: Entrepreneurs have the flexibility to set their own schedules, work from home and create a work/life balance that suites them.

iv. **Financial reward**: They can be financially rewarded if successful, offering potential for significant returns on investment.

v. **Personal growth**: Being an entrepreneur requires personal growth and development, as you learn new skills, overcome challenges and gain experience.

vi. **Control**: You have control over your business and can shape its direction and culture.

vii. **Job creation**: Entrepreneurs create jobs and contribute to the economy by building successful businesses.

viii.   **Legacy**: Building a successful business can create a lasting legacy that can benefit future generations.

ix.   **Sense of purpose**: Many entrepreneurs find a sense of purpose and fulfillment in creating and building something from scratch.

1.6 CREATIVITY AND INNOVATION IN ENTREPRENEURSHIP

Definitions

- **Creativity:** refers to the ability of entrepreneurs to develop new and original ideas and solutions to problems.

  It involves using imagination and innovation to creatively approach traditional business practices, products or services in order to provide something unique and valuable to customers.

- **Innovation:** refers to the process of bringing new ideas, products, services or processes to the market.

  It involves creating something that is new and different also adding value to the customers, society or the business itself.

  Examples of how creativity and innovation can be applied in entrepreneurship;

  Developing new products or services, disrupting established markets, improving existing products, creating a unique brand, finding new markets, solving complex problems among others.

1.7 IMPORTANCE OF CREATIVITY IN BUSINESS

Creativity is essential in business for several reasons;

i. **Innovation**: Creative ideas are a starting point for developing new products, services and technologies that can help businesses stay competitive and meet evolving customer needs.

ii. **Problem-solving**: Creativity helps businesses solve complex problems in unique and innovative ways. Creative thinking encourages employees to approach problems in new and different ways, to find solutions that others may have overlooked.

iii. **Marketing**: Creative and engaging marketing campaigns can capture people's attention and help businesses reach new customers or retain existing ones.

iv. **Efficiency**: Creative thinking can help businesses streamline processes and improve efficiency, reducing overall production costs and increasing profitability.

v. **Employee engagement**: Employees who are engaged in creative projects are more likely to feel valued and motivated to stay with the company long term.

1.8 HOW TO BECOME CREATIVE

Some ways to become more creative as an entrepreneur are as follows;

i. **Keep an open mind**: Be open to new ideas and perspectives. This means being willing to listen to others, even if their ideas conflict with your own.

ii. **Take risks**: Don't be afraid to try new things and don't be discouraged if some of your ideas don't work out.

iii. **Embrace failure**: Failure is an essential part of the creative process. Don't be afraid to fail and don't let failures discourage you from trying again.

iv. **Practice creativity**: Make time to practice thinking and problem solving regularly, whether it's through brain-storming sessions, mind mapping or other creative exercises.

v. **Seek-out inspirations**: Look for inspiration from a variety of sources such as books, podcasts, documentaries and even the natural world around you.

vi. **Collaborate**: Work with others who have different skills and perspectives, and encourage team members to share their ideas openly.

vii. **Stay curious**: Always ask questions, be curious about the world around you and seek out new knowledge and experiences.

1.9 INNOVATION IN BUSINESS

Definition

Refers to the process of introducing new ideas, methods, products or services that create value for customers, improve operational efficiency and drive growth and profitability for the organization.

It involves creating and implementing new ways of doings things that different from current methods and which offer an advantage over competitors or address the needs of customers in a better way.

Innovation can be incremental, involving small improvements to existing products or services.

1.10 TYPES OF INNOVATION

There are several types of innovation as follows;

i.   **Product innovation**: Involves creating new or improved products or services which can be a result of advanced technology, better materials or processes, or new functionality.

ii. **Process innovation**: Involves optimizing or streamlining existing processes to reduce costs, improve quality or increase productivity.

iii. **Marketing innovation**: Involves creating new ways to market and promote products or services that can include new channels, messaging and branding.

iv. **Business model innovation**: Involves creating new business models or modifying existing ones, to better align with customer needs or changing market conditions.

v. **Organizational innovation**: Involves creating new structures, processes and culture within an organization, to enhance efficiency, collaboration and agility.

vi. **Social innovation**: Involves creating new solutions to social problems or addressing unmet social needs, which can result in positive societal impact and financial returns.

1.11 IMPORTANCE OF INNOVATION

Innovation is a key driver and entrepreneurs able to innovate and find new ways of doing things are more likely to succeed, grow and make impact in the world.

Here are some main reasons why innovation is important in entrepreneurship;

i. **Staying competitive**: Helps entrepreneurs stay ahead of their competitors by developing products or services that are better or different from anything else on the market.

ii. **Meeting customer needs**: Innovation allows entrepreneurs to identify and address unmet customer needs which can be a key driver of success in many industries.

iii. **Increasing profits**: Innovation can result in new or improved products or services can lead to increased revenues and profitability which is essential for the long-term success of any business.

iv. **Attracting investors**: Innovations can be compelling to investors, who often seek out entrepreneurs and start-ups that are doing something unique and cutting-edge.

v. **Creating impact**: Entrepreneurs who innovate can make a positive impact on society by providing products or services that improve peoples' lives, create jobs or address pressing social issues.

1.12 HOW TO BECOME INNOVATIVE/FEATURES OF AN INNOVATOR

i. **Identify a problem**: in a particular industry or market that you're interested in. This can be an opportunity for you to come up with innovative solutions that may not have been considered before.

ii. **Study the market**: Research the industry and understand needs and preferences of target audience. By doing so, you can identify new opportunities for innovation.

iii. **Collaborate with others**: Partner with like-minded individuals, businesses or organizations to exchange ideas, resources and expertise.

iv. **Experiment and take risks**: Don't be afraid to try new things and take risks.

v. **Keep an eye on emerging technologies and trends**: Stay up-to-date on emerging technologies, trends and industry developments. This can help you identify new opportunities for innovation and stay ahead of competitors.

vi. **Seek feedback**: Get feedback from potential customers, investors and colleagues to gauge the viability and potential impact of your ideas. This feedback also helps you refine and improve your innovation.

vii. **Continually iterate**: Continually revise and improve your ideas, products or services based on feedback and changes in the market.

1.13 RISKS IN BUSINESS

Risks are an inherent part of business and every decision business owner makes involves some level of risk

1.14 MEANING OF RISKS

Definition

Risk refers to potential hazards, uncertainties and negative outcomes that businesses may face when making strategic, operational or financial decisions.

These risks can arise from a range of factors, like internal factors such as poor management, inadequate human resources and over reliance on a single client or external factors such as downturns, natural disasters and regulatory changes.

1.15 TYPES OF RISKS

Here are some types of risks faced by entrepreneurs;

i. **Financial risks**: An entrepreneur invests capital in their venture, in the hope of generating profits. There is a possibility of losing the invested capital and not earning any returns.

ii. **Market risks**: Entrepreneurs taking risks by introducing new products or services to the market which may or may not be accepted by the target audience.

iii. **Operational risks**: Daily operations of a business involves risks such as equipment failure, supply chain disruptions, human error and cyber threats.

iv. **Legal risks**: Entrepreneurs must comply with laws and regulations to avoid legal implications. Failure to comply can lead to fines or lawsuits.

v. **Reputational risk**: Credibility of a business can be impacted by negative feedback, scandals or public relations crises leading to damage to the brand and loss of customers.

vi. **Human resource risks**: Employment related risks can arise from factors like employee turn-over, inadequate workforce or lack of training and development.

vii. **Personal risks**: Entrepreneurs often invest their personal savings, time and effort into building their businesses. Any failure can result in a personal loss of reputation, credit and savings.

1.16 THE RISK-TAKING GAME

Can help entrepreneurs learn, identify, assess and manage risks in a fun and interactive way. Here are some ideas on how to create a risk-taking game;

i. **Brainstorm potential risks**: Gather a group of entrepreneurs and brainstorm potential risks that they may face, such as financial risk etc.

ii. **Assign value to risks**: Assign a point value to each risk based on its level of severity. For example, a high financial risk may be worth more points than a low operational risk.

iii. **Create scenarios**: that involve different risks and assign them point values based on the risks involved.

iv. **Play the game**: Divide players into teams and have them take turns choosing a scenario. Players must then decide whether to take the risk and try to achieve the outcome, or to avoid the risk and settle for a smaller reward.

v. **Award points**: to each team based on the decision they made and the outcome of their choice.

1.17 ASSESSING RISKS

Assessing risks is a critical process for entrepreneurs as it helps in identifying potential threats and developing strategies to mitigate them. Here are some steps to assess risks in entrepreneurship;

i. **Identify risks**: Start by identifying potential risks in your business. Consider competition, staff turnover among others.

ii. **Analyze risks**: including the likelihood of occurrence and the potential impact on your business.

iii. **Prioritize risks**: based on the likelihood of occurrence and potential impact they could have on your businesses. This will help you focus on high priority risks when developing risk mitigation strategies.

iv. **Develop risk mitigation strategies**: for each of the high priority risks. This can include developing contingency plans, increasing insurance coverage, diversifying your product offerings.

v. **Monitor and review risks**: revising your mitigation strategies as needed. This ensures that you are always up-to-date with the changing business landscape and are prepared for any potential risks.

1.18 RISK MANAGEMENT IN BUSINESS

Definition

Risk management refers to the process of identifying, assessing and controlling risk that could potentially impact a business negatively.

It is important for businesses to effectively manage risks as it helps them make informed decisions, minimize losses and maximize opportunities.

1.19 TECHNOLOGY AND BUSINESS

Technology has had a tremendous impact on the world of business, leading to significant changes in the way that businesses operate and compete. Here are some few ways that technology has transformed business;

i. **Increased efficiency**: Technology has enabled businesses to automate routine tasks, leading to increased efficiency in operations. **For example**, businesses can use software to manage inventory, process orders and shipments, and handle customer inquiries.

ii. **Improved communications**: Technology has made communication faster and more efficient. Businesses can now communicate with customers and employees through email, instant messaging, video conferencing and other digital channels.

iii. **Enhanced customer experience**: such as personalized recommendations and 24/7 customer support. **For example**, e-commerce platforms can use data analytics to provide tailored recommendations to customers based on their browsing and purchases history.

iv. **Increased competitiveness**: Technology has leveled the ground allowing smaller businesses to compete with larger ones. Digital advertising, social media and e-commerce platforms have made it easier for businesses to reach new customers and expand their market reach.

v. **Innovation and new business models**: Technology has enabled new business models to emerge like software as a service (SaaS) and subscription-based models like Netflix .

1.20 MEANING OF E-BUSINESS

Definition

Also known as electronic business, refers to any business activity that is conducted online or through digital channels.

Includes buying and selling products and services, digital marketing and advertising, online customer service, and online data management.

E-business typically involves use of websites, mobile apps, social media and other digital technologies to facilitate business transactions and interactions with customers.

The goal for e-business is to improve efficiency, reduce costs and expand a business's reach by leveraging digital technologies.

1.21 DOING E-BUSINESS

E-business involves several components as follows;

i. **Online presence**: An e-business needs a website or an online storefront that serves as its primary interface with customers.

ii. **Digital marketing**: techniques like search engine optimization(SEO), social media marketing(SMM), and email marketing to drive traffic to their websites.

iii. **E-commerce platform**: to provide infrastructure for online sale of goods and services like online catalogs, shopping carts among others.

iv. **Online customer service**: through online channels like email, chat and social media.

v. **Data analysis**: E-businesses need to track and analyze customer behavior and online sales data to make informed business decisions.

1.22 BENEFITS/ADVANTAGES OF E-BUSINESS TO AN ENTREPRENEUR

E-business provides several advantages to entrepreneurs, including;

i. **Lower overhead costs**: Compared to traditional brick and mortar businesses, e-businesses require lower startup costs and lower ongoing operational costs.

ii.   **Global reach**: E-businesses can reach customers worldwide, allowing entrepreneurs to expand their customer base beyond their local area.

iii.   **Increased sales potential**: With an online presence, e-businesses can operate 24/7, allowing them to reach customer even when traditional businesses are closed.

iv.   **Improved customer engagement**: Can use digital marketing tools to engage with customers on a more personalized level, building better relationships.

v.   **Data-driven decision-making**: E-business data analytics provide valuable insight into customer behavior, purchase patterns and sales trends, enabling entrepreneurs to make data-driven decisions.

vi.   **Scalability**: with increased sales , e-businesses can easily scale their operations.

1.23 CHALLENGES OF USING E-BUSINESS

Although e-businesses offer many advantages, they also come with some challenges which include;

i.   **Competition**: with many other businesses vying for the same customers.

ii. **Security concerns**: E-businesses must take measures to secure their online transactions, including the use of encryption and secure payment portals, to protect customer information and prevent cyber attacks.

iii. **Technical issues**: such as website crashes or server downtimes can impact sales and customer satisfaction.

iv. **Shipping logistics**: E-businesses need to handle orders, shipping and delivery of physical products, which can be complicated, require additional resources and fast delivery expectations.

v. **Trust concerns**: Customers might have difficulty trusting an e-business, particularly if it is a new or unknown entity.

EXERCISE

a. Who is an entrepreneur?

b. Outline the purposes of entrepreneurship education in Uganda

c. Define entrepreneurship

d. State at-least four characteristics of an entrepreneur.

e. What are different benefits of being an entrepreneur nowadays in Uganda?

f. Differentiate between creativity and innovation.

g. How can one become creative in the field of entrepreneurship?

h. Define innovation

i. Give three types of innovation

j. Outline five features of an innovator

k. Define risks in business

l. State any two types of risks

m. Create a scenario on risk-taking

n. How can we assess risks in an enterprise?

o. What is risk management?

p. Write short notes on technology and business

q. What does e-business mean?

r. Discuss different pros and cons of e-business to the entrepreneur

Chapter 2

Businesses In Uganda

2.1 TYPES OF BUSINESSES

There are different types/ kinds of businesses, as follows;

i. **Sole proprietorship**: This is when a business is owned and operated by one person. **Examples** include a freelance writing business or a mobile car wash service.

ii. **Partnership**: This is where two or more people own a business together. They share in the profits and losses. **Examples** include a law firm or a restaurant owned by two friends.

iii. **Limited liability company (LLC)**: This a type of business that combines elements of both a partnership and a corporation. This means that the owners have some liability protection, but the business is still taxed like a partnership. An **example** is a small restaurant chain.

iv. **Corporation**: This is a separate legal entity from the owners. A corporation can own property and enter into contracts. **Examples** include a large retail chain or a technology company.

v. **Cooperative**: This is when a group of people work together to own and operate a business. This means that the profits are shared among the owners, who are also employees. An **example** is a bike-sharing company.

vi. **Franchise**: This is where a business owner allows another person to use their brand name and business model in exchange for a fee. **Examples** include a fast-food chain like KFC or hotel chain.

vii. **Non-profit organizations**: Is a business that does not aim to make profit. Instead, it focuses on serving a specific purpose or cause. **Examples** include a charity or a religious organization.

viii. **Joint venture**: Is when two or more businesses work together to achieve a specific goal or project. **Example** might be when a car manufacturer joins forces with a tech company to create a self-driving car.

ix. **S Corporation**: Is a special type of corporation that allows the owners to avoid double taxation. This means that the profits are only taxed once at the individual level. An **example** might be a small accounting firm.

x. **Small business**: Is one independently owned and operated and has a small number of employees. **Examples** include a family-owned restaurant or a local boutique.

2.2 MEANING OF BUSINESS

- Business is a very important term that is used to describe many different activities that people engage in everyday to make money.

- A business is an organization that is involved in the production or sale of goods and services to make a profit.

- A business activity that is designed to create a product or service that people want or need, and then sell that product or service to customers at a price that is higher than the cost of producing it.

- The difference between the price and cost is the profit that the business makes, which is the main goal of any business.

- There are different types of businesses, from small family-run businesses to large multinational corporations

- Some businesses are based on providing a service, such as hair salon or a cash wash, while others are based on producing a product like toys or computers.

- Starting a business can be difficult but a lot of things need to be considered like creating a business plan, securing funding, and attracting customers.

- However owning and operating a successful business can be very rewarding, both financially and personally.

- In addition, businesses can also have a great impact on society like creating jobs and providing goods and services that make people's lives easier or more enjoyable.

- Overall, business is a very important part of the economy and our daily lives.

2.3 SUCCESS IN BUSINESS

To succeed in a business, there are a few things you need to keep in mind. Here are some tips that can help you;

i. Have a good idea: You need a good idea for a product or service that people want or need. Think of something that you're passionate about or that solves a problem.

ii. Determine your target audience: Once you have your idea, you need to understand who your target audience is. Who are the people that would be interested in your product or service?

iii. Develop a business plan: A business plan is like a roadmap for your business. It outlines your goals, how you'll reach them, and how you'll measure success.

iv. Secure funding: Starting a business can be expensive. You may need to secure funding from investors, a bank, or other sources to get started.

v.   Market your business: You need to get your name out there and let people know about your product or service. Develop a marketing plan that targets your ideal customers.

vi.   Provide excellent customer service: Customer service is key to any successful business. Treat your customers well and they'll keep coming back.

vii.   Be flexible and willing to learn: Business is constantly changing, so you need to be flexible and willing to adapt to new challenges. Keep learning and growing and don't be afraid to make changes when necessary.

A few start-ups in Uganda include safeboda, tubayo etc.

EXERCISE

a. Define business

b. Outline at-least ten types of businesses

c. How can one succeed in the business world?

d. What is the full form of LLC?

Chapter 3

Business Ideas and Business Opportunities

3.1 BUSINESS IDEAS

Definition

These are simply plans or thoughts for products or services that can sell in exchange for money. **For example**, if I had an idea for a cool t-shirt design and decided to sell t-shirts with that design on them, that would be a business idea.

The possibilities for business ideas are endless, and can come from something you're passionate about, a problem you want to solve, or a need that you've noticed in your community.

The key is finding something that people will want to buy and that you'll enjoy doing.

Once you have a business idea, you need to think about things like how much you'll sell it for, how much it will cost to make, how you'll market it to the people.

The more you research and plan, the more likely your business idea will turn into a successful business.

Types of business ideas

Here are some common types of business ideas;

i.   **Product-based business ideas**: This is one that sells a physical product like clothing or jewelry. You could make the product yourself, or purchase it at wholesale to sell in your own store or online.

ii.   **Service-based business ideas**: This is one that provides a service like house cleaning or money lending. You would offer your skills or expertise to people who need it, and charge a fee for your services.

iii.   **Online-based business ideas**: This is one that operates solely online like a blog or online store. You would need to create a website to sell your products or services and promote it through social media or other online marketing strategies.

iv.   **Social enterprise business ideas**: This is one that aims at making social impact as well as a profit. **For example** you could start a business that sells eco-friendly products or donates a percentage of sales to charity.

v.   **Franchise business ideas**: This is one where you purchase the rights to use a proven business model and brand name like KFC. You would then run a franchise location of the business and earn a percentage of profits.

Sources of business ideas

Here are some different sources of business ideas that might help get you inspired;

i.   **Problem-solving**: Sometimes the best business ideas come from identifying a problem or need that hasn't been met yet. You could think about common issues in everyday life or possible gaps in the market that you could fill.

ii.   **Passion**: Many successful businesses are started by people who have a strong personal interest or passion for a product or service. For example, if you love baking, you could create a bakery or start a home-based baking business.

iii.   **Innovation**: Sometimes businesses create entirely new products or services that are unlike anything else on the market. Think about what's missing that could make things easier or more convenient , or efficient.

iv.   **Industry trend**: You can also examine current trends in a particular industry or fields to identify potential business ideas. For example if you're into fashion and notice that a lot of celebs are wearing hats, you could start selling them online.

v.   **Personal experience**: Perhaps you have lived through a personal experience, such as a health issue, that has made you passionate about helping other people navigate the same situation. You could start a business that provides support and resources to others in similar situations.

Remember, the key to a successful business idea is that it meets a need or solves a problem, so keep an eye out for opportunities.

3.2 MARKET SURVEY

Definition

A market survey is a way of finding out what people think about a product or a service by asking them questions. It's like when you want to know what game your friends like to play, so you ask them.

But instead of asking your friends, you ask a lot of people and ask them specific questions to understand what they like or don't like about the product or service.

The survey usually consists of a series of questions, and people can answer them in different ways such as "yes" or "no" questions or multiple-choice questions.

Process of conducting a market survey

The process of a market survey involves a few steps;

- First, you need to figure out what you want to know. For example, if you're planning to start a new business, you may want to know what your potential customers like or dislike about your product idea.

- Next, you need to decide who you want to ask. You might want to survey people who fit your target customer demographic, like age or location.

- Then, you need to design your survey questions. You want to ask questions that are easy to understand, and that will give you the information you want. Sometimes, you can use a pre-made survey template or tools to help you create the questions.

- Once you have your questions designed, you need to ask people to take the survey. You can do this in different ways like using email, social media or in-person events.

- After you collect the responses to your survey, you need to analyze the information you received. You can use different tools to make sense of the data, such as charts or graphs. This will help you understand your potential customers' preferences better

- Finally, you need to use insights from your market survey to make decisions about your business idea such as adjusting your product offering or changing your marketing strategy.

Different market survey tools

There are different kinds of survey tools that you can use to conduct a market survey;

i. **Online surveys**: You can use tools such as google forms, SurveyMonkey, or Typeform to create your survey questions, and then send a link via email, social media or your website.

ii. **Phone surveys**: You can use tools such as google voice or skype if you want to make international calls

iii. **In-person surveys**: You can also conduct surveys by going where you target audience is and asking them to answer your survey questions in person.

iv. **Focus groups**: This is a group interview where you can get insights from multiple people at once. You bring a group of people together, ask them questions and then record their responses. You can use tools like zoom or skype.

v. **Social media monitoring**: You can monitor conversations on social media listening tools like Mention or Hootsuite to automate this process.

EXERCISE

a. Define a business idea

b. What are some of the different sources of business ideas?

c. Explain four types of business ideas

d. What is a market survey?

e. Outline the process of conducting a market survey

f. Discuss few survey tools used in the market.

Chapter 4

The Business Start-Up Process

4.1 STEPS IN STARTING A BUSINESS

Starting a business might seem like a big task, but it is not as complicated as you think. Here are the different steps involved in starting a business;

a. **Come up with a good business idea**: The first step in starting a business is to find a great business idea that you are passionate about. Think about your strengths, interests and skills to come up with a unique business idea that you can pursue.

b. **Create a business plan**: A business plan is like a blueprint or roadmap for the future of your business. It outlines your business idea, target audience, marketing plan, and financial plan. A good business plan will help you to stay organized and focused while getting started.

c. **Choose a business structure**: Different types of business structures include sole proprietorship, LLC, corporation, and cooperatives. Choose a business structure that suits your needs and goals.

d. **Register your business**: You will need to register your business with the government, depending on your location and business structure. This process requires you to obtain specific licenses and permits, depending on your industry and location.

e. **Choose a business**: Your business name is essential for making a first impression on your customers. Choose a name that reflects your business goals and brand image.

f. **Set up a business location**: You may need to rent or purchase a location to carry out your business operations. Ensure you conduct thorough research on different locations before choosing one that meets your needs.

g. **Hire staff**: You may need to hire staff depending on your business needs. Hire people who are skilled, reliable and trustworthy.

h. **Create a marketing plan**: Creating a marketing plan is crucial for promoting your business and attracting customers. Your plan may include advertising, social media presence, and search engine optimization.

Different bodies to help register businesses and workers in Uganda include Uganda Registration Services Bureau (URSB), National Social Security Fund (NSSF).

4.2 SAVING AND INVESTMENT

Saving and investing are two concepts that are essential to achieving financial stability and success.

Firstly, let's understand what saving means. **Saving** is the process of putting aside a portion of your income for future use. This can include short-term savings, like saving for college, or a car.

Saving money is crucial because it helps you to be prepared for emergencies and gives you the freedom to achieve your goals.

To start saving, create a budget that outlines your expenses and income. Determine a realistic amount that you can set aside each month and stick to it.

Next, let's look at investing. **Investing** is the process of putting your money into an asset with the expectation of earning a profit from it. This can include stocks, bonds, mutual funds or real estate.

Investing can be riskier than saving because there is a chance of losing money. However, investing has the potential of earning higher returns than savings accounts.

To start investing, research different investment options and determine your risk tolerance. Always invest in a diversified portfolio, which means investing in different types of assets to spread your risk.

4.3 LOCATION OF A BUSINESS

General guidelines on what factors to consider when choosing a location for your business;

i. **Accessibility**: A business location should be easily accessible for both employees and customers. Look for locations that are close to highways, public transportation, and ample parking options.

ii.   **Demographics**: Consider the demographics of the neighborhood where you want to open your business. Look for locations that have a large population of your target audience.

iii.   **Competition**: Take note of the competition in the area. Are there already similar businesses operating in the same location? If so, it might be best to consider a different location with less competition.

iv.   **Rent and utilities**: The cost of renting and utilities can vary depending on the location. Look for a location that fits your budget and offers favorable terms.

v.   **Future development**: Consider the area's growth potential. Is there new construction or planned developments? A location that is growing can be beneficial for your business in the long-run.

EXERCISE

a. Outline eight steps of starting a business.

b. Write short notes about saving and investing.

c. What are the factors that affect the location of a business?

Chapter 5

Government Revenue

5.1 INTRODUCTION TO GOVERNMENT REVENUE

Definition

Government revenue refers to money earned by the government through various sources like taxes, fees, fines, licenses, and other forms of payments.

This revenue is used to fund government programs and services, such as education, healthcare, defense, transportation, and social welfare programs.

Government revenue is crucial to maintaining the functioning of the government and providing for the needs of the citizens.

Sources of government revenue

There are different sources of government revenue including;

i. **Taxes**: This includes income taxes, sales taxes, property taxes and corporate taxes.

ii. **Fees**: Government charges fees for services like issuing passports, driver's license and other licenses and permits.

iii. **Fines**: Traffic tickets, parking tickets, and other fines are a source of revenue for governments.

iv. **Lottery**: Revenue earned from lottery sales is also considered as a source of government revenue.

v. **Bonds**: The government issues bonds to raise funds from investors, which it later repays with interest.

vi. **Investment income**: This includes income earned from investing in stocks, bonds, and other securities.

vii. **Monopoly rents**: Revenue earned from state-owned enterprise like oil & gas and utilities.

viii. **Grants and aid**: Revenue received from foreign countries, international organizations, and other entities in the form of aid and grants.

ix. **Borrowing**: Governments can borrow money from individuals, financial institutions, and other countries.

Importance of the government to businesses in Uganda

Some of the key importance of government to business are;

i. **Creating a conducive business environment**: The government creates and implements policies and regulations that create a favorable business environment for local and foreign investors. For example, the government has implemented various policies that encourage entrepreneurship, such as tax concessions, subsidies, and streamlined business registration procedures.

ii. **Providing infrastructure**: The government invests in infrastructure development, such as roads, electricity, water supply and telecommunications, which are essential for the growth of businesses. By providing reliable basic infrastructure services, the government facilitates the growth and expansion of businesses in Uganda.

iii. **Facilitating trade**: The government's trade policies and agreements with other countries are critical in facilitating trade for Ugandan businesses both domestically and internationally.

iv. **Maintaining social stability**: The government plays a crucial role in maintaining social stability, enforcing the rule of law, and ensuring the security of businesses and their property. Social stability is essential for businesses to run efficiently in Uganda.

v. **Provision of finance**: The government also helps businesses access finance and financial services through its development finance institutions and initiatives.

Overall, the government's role is vital in creating a conducive, stable, and predictable business environment in Uganda that supports sustainable growth, job creation, and national development.

EXERCISE

a. Give brief notes about government revenue

b. What are some sources of government revenue?

c. State the importance of government to businesses in Uganda.